ONE SHOT: A UNIQUE OPTIONS TRADING STRATEGY

A SINGLE STRATEGY TO TRADE INDEX & STOCK OPTIONS

K SAURABH

Copyright © K Saurabh
All Rights Reserved.

ISBN 978-1-64951-464-6

This book has been published with all efforts taken to make the material error-free after the consent of the author. However, the author and the publisher do not assume and hereby disclaim any liability to any party for any loss, damage, or disruption caused by errors or omissions, whether such errors or omissions result from negligence, accident, or any other cause.

While every effort has been made to avoid any mistake or omission, this publication is being sold on the condition and understanding that neither the author nor the publishers or printers would be liable in any manner to any person by reason of any mistake or omission in this publication or for any action taken or omitted to be taken or advice rendered or accepted on the basis of this work. For any defect in printing or binding the publishers will be liable only to replace the defective copy by another copy of this work then available.

Contents

Preface	v
Prologue	vii
1. Let's Talk The "loss" First	1
2. Options & Their Types	3
3. Trading Strategy For Index Options	6
4. Trading The Stock Options In The Month Expiry	10
Risk Disclaimer	13

Preface

Over the years OPTIONS as a trading instrument in the Stock Market has gained a lot of popularity because of its rewarding factor. But, nothing comes handy when you enter the live trade. You might have heard from the professional traders, that option buyers mostly end up losing money while options writers (Sellers of the option) gain and the reason they provide for such instance is the decay value of the contract with time. I am not ruling out anyone's statement rather my aim is just to chnage this myth by introducing to you all a very simple and efficient option trading strategy which literally will require no prerequisites or trading skills.

However, the choice is yours, whether you want to devote time and money to gain competency in your trade by learning lots of complex theories or you want to make it simple just by reading few pages in which I will be sharing my personal trading strategy.

Before we begin, let me introduce myself to you. My name is Saurabh and I started my trading journey in the Indian Stock Market in March 2017. At that time I was not even familiar with the ABC of the stock trading but I managed to device trading strategies with time which now keeps me confident while taking any trade in the live market and at the same time the trading results remain fruitful.

The idea behind writing this book is only to help out such traders who have lost immense amount of their money by trying different things and yet the outcome is zero or inconsistent trading results. So, whether you are a novice trader, a struggling day trader, an intermediate skilled trader or even if you are a professional, I would recommend you to read my book.

PREFACE

I am pretty sure, you won't regret investing your time and money. Get your hands on practically observed and proven strategies, a result oriented **"Option Trading Strategy"** that will change the way you look at options.

Prologue

"The History Repeats Itself" A popularly used statement in context of the stock market, as we see the price trends setting up the same pattern which were observed earlier as well. My unique option trading strategy is no different from this statement. I have traded in stock and index options since October 2017 and so far whenever I come across that chart pattern, I see the history repeating with a strike rate of over 90% and that is the the reason I myself call it "The Magical Pattern". I find it no less than a "Holy Grail".

Getting started to trade options and a willingness to be a pro is really a good vision but how many traders actually reach to this level? I think, the trading success statistics is not hidden from anyone. Well, let me first talk about some of the high profile trading terms used in options. The terms such as Alpha, Gamma, Theta Decay, Bull Call Spread, Bull Put

Spread, Synthetic Long & Arbitrage, The Long Straddle, The Short Straddle and much more, oh really! Do we need to learn these all to become a successful option trader? May be! But, my point of view believes in simplifying the complexities. What if I tell you, that, for making a profitable trade in options, I just need a naked chart with simple candlesticks, no additional indicators! What if I require only 8 trading sessions and can enjoy the rest of the days in comfort! Sounds quite impossible, Right? No pal, it's not!

So, whether you have a losing capacity of few hundreds or lakhs or crores, just get to know this simple approach to trade options. No matter what your skill level is, a beginner, novice or advanced. It will help every single trader. If it works for me, it will work for you too, irrespective of the geographical boundaries and Stock Markets. Now, let us get started with learning one simple strategy to ease the way you traded options, this is the very reason, I named it "One Shot".

CHAPTER ONE

Let's Talk The "Loss" First

Before getting started as a trader in the stock market, it is very important to undersatnd the risk. Those who have already been associated with the stock strading must be very well aware of the risks involved in trading stocks.

The topic "Risk Management", like different trading techniques has lot to talk about, but as I said, I like things to be simple. So, when you finally decide to enter into the trading in stock markets, just take care of one thing, that is, do not exceed your losing limit.

To put it simple, let say you have the capacity to lose a sum of Rupee 1,000 in a month, that means even if you lose it, nothing is going to impact you, neither your budget is going to be affected nor you will incur any financial crisis. Therefore, you can put this amount of money at stake in your trades. Consider the another case, in this case if you lose 1,050 Rupees in the market, then it will directly or indirectly impact your budget or might lead to tensions. So, never ever you will exceed or put at stake even a single penny more than what you can afford to lose. Remain sticked to this rule, the time will make you a better trader.

The another important thing to keep in mind is, the ongoing opportunity is not the end of the opportunity, that is, if you have missed a great trading opportunity, it does not mean that you won't get another, of course you will. So, don't be impatient while trading in the stock market.

This was just a brush up, now let us get to the real task!

CHAPTER TWO

Options & Their Types

As you would be learning to trade in stock and index options, so let us first get an overview. one of the most popular trading instruments in the stock market, called "The Options" are of two different types:

1. The Call options
2. The Put options

The value of a call option rises when the stock or the corresponding index rises in price and vice-versa. Likewise, the value of a put option rises when the corresponding stock or the index value falls down considerably. That is, it works just opposite of the call option. Again, there is a term, In The Money & Out of The Money Options. Let's make it simple, whether it is a put option or the call option, the in the money option will always have a greater value whereas, if an option is out of the money, its value will be comparatively lower than in the money options.

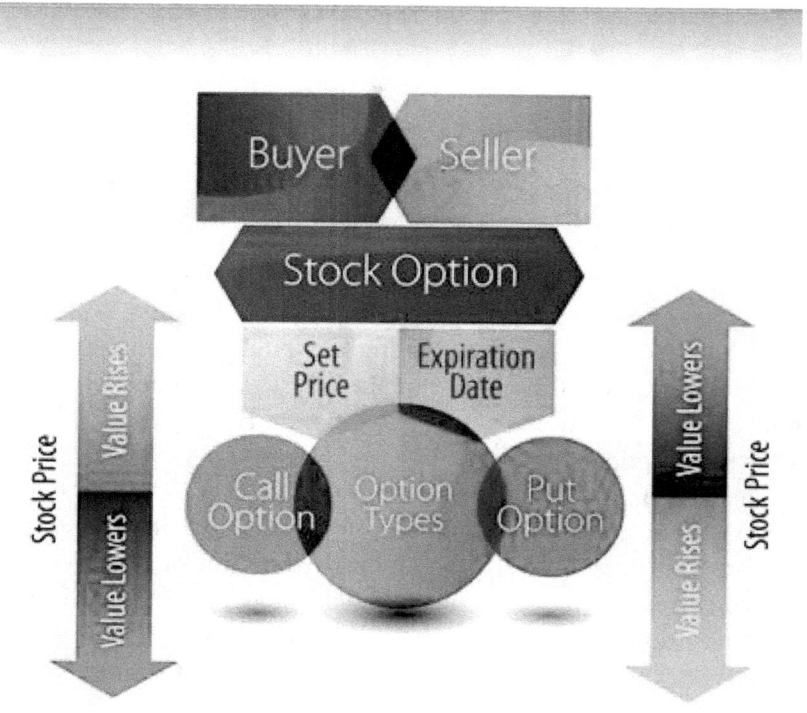

Before getting into these, first understand the strike price, let say the Nifty 50 is trading at 10,900, then 11000,11050,11100,10850,10800,10750,10600, etc. all these prices will be known as strike price, that is the price points below or above a certain asset, whether that is a stock or index, is referred to as strike price. Now, for example if Indusind Bank is trading at 520, then 500, 480, 460, etc. these price points will be termed as in the money call options, as their value is below the stock's current price, while 540, 560, etc. will be out of the money call options. The put option is just the opposite, that is price points above the stock's current price are said to be in the money put options, while price points below the assest's price are known as out of the money put options. I just briefed a bit, however I assume that you already are familiar with these terms. Even if you are unaware of these, this small information which has been given here is sufficient for you to get started with the trading.

Also remember, the put option value will rise if the stock or index is considerably negative while the call option will be seen to rise if the market has a positive momentum. Call options are represented by CE and put options are represented by PE. All these stock and Index options have a fixed date on which they expire, which we call the monthly and the weekly expiry and this is the day when you will be trading using the strategy which will be discussed in the next chapter.

CHAPTER THREE

Trading Strategy For Index Options

There are many indices in the market, however, the most traded option contracts belong to Nifty 50 and the Bank Nifty. Both these indices contains certain set of stock with individual weightages, the rise and fall of those stocks contribute to the rise and fall of these Nifty and Bank Nifty index. You should be aware that the option contract of these indices expire on weekly basis, on every thursday, only in rare cases the expiry will take place on Wednesday, if there is a National Holiday.

Now, what is the strategy and how we will trade using these? So, just few things have to be kept in mind and a single chart pattern. These things will give you a clear view regarding what to buy, a call or a put!

Pay special attention to the following set of conditions which must satisfy, only upon these conditions are met, we can decide about trading a call or a put option.

Selection of Trading: Call or Put

We will buy call on Thursday around 1 to 2:45 PM if:

- Beginning from the last week's Friday, the Bank Nifty recorded a fall of at least 1000 points
- The value of the call is somewhere between 1.5 to 10 rupees
- The distance of the call option is at around 200 to 300 points above the value of the Bank Nifty
- The final decision to take the trade will be executed only if the chart pattern is exactly the same which is shown below

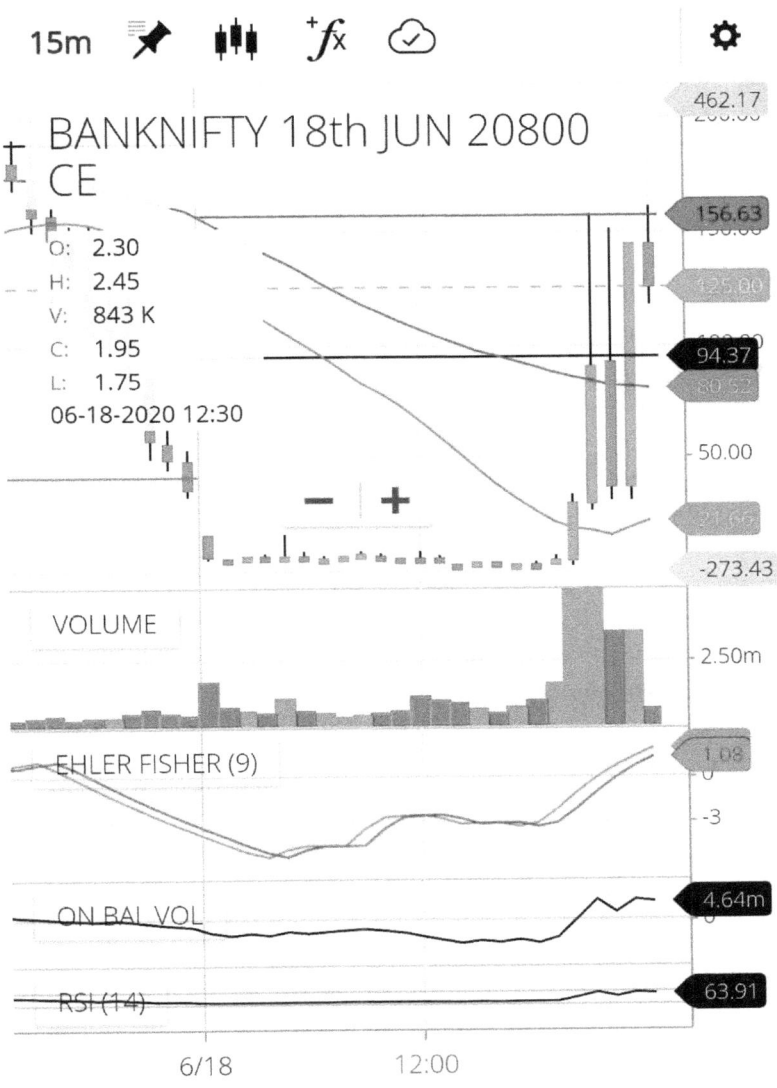

Look at the chart pattern carefully, you do not need to focus on other technical patterns, just watch the candlestick formation, keep the time frame 15 minutes on the chart and see if you are able to observe the alternate red and green small dotted pattern. If yes, then go for taking the trade, if no, then avoid trading for that particular day. The same thing applies with trading put options too, but set of conditions will be a little

ONE SHOT: A UNIQUE OPTIONS TRADING STRATEGY

different. Remember, that the set of conditions only give us a perception but the actual trade is made based upon the chart pattern only. So, whether to trade or not will completely be decided by observing the chart pattern.

We will buy put on Thursday around 1 to 2:45 PM if:

- Beginning from the last week's Friday, the BankNifty recorded a rise of at least 1000 points
- The value of the put is somewhere between 1.5 to 10 rupees
- The distance of the put option is at around 200 to 300 points below the value of the Bank Nifty
- The final decision to take the trade will be executed only if the chart pattern is exactly the same which is shown above

How Much Quantity To Buy & What To Expect From The Trade:

On Thursday, whether you are trading Nifty options or Bank Nifty options, just remember that a chart pattern as shown above must appear in the last trading hours, that is 1 or 1 & 1/2 Hour before the market's closing time, which is 3:30 PM. If you are trading Nifty's call or put, the strike price's distance should not be more than 50-100 points distant from the Nifty's current value and their price must be somewhere around 1 to 3 Rupees, likewise if you are trading Bank Nifty options, do not forget to keep in mind the above mentioned criterias.

Now, the number of lots, that means the shares that you will buy, will depend upon the amount of money that is there with you which you can easily afford to lose. Let say if you have Rupees 500 to lose, then buy 60 quantities of Bank Nifty options at around 7-8 Rupees, place a sell limit order of 40 quantities at 18-19 Rupees, that is 10 points above, and the rest 20 quantity you can keep for capturing huge move that could be around 50 or 100 points up from your buying price. This is the general observation about which I am talking based upon my past experiences, even the above chart is not too old, it was captured on 18th June 2020. However, you can not take things for granted, that is why, take partial profits, and then enjoy the ride. Sometimes, if the market behaves in a rangebound manner, you might end up making losses.

The Magical Chart Pattern:

The reason I call this a magical pattern is because, starting from October 2017 till date, whenever I have seen such chart formation taking place,

I have been able to capture the huge moves in option. Literally, it never ditched me. So, forget all the technicals, just observe in the chart and see if you are able to see these alternate red and green small dotted candlestick patterns? If yes, the day is yours!

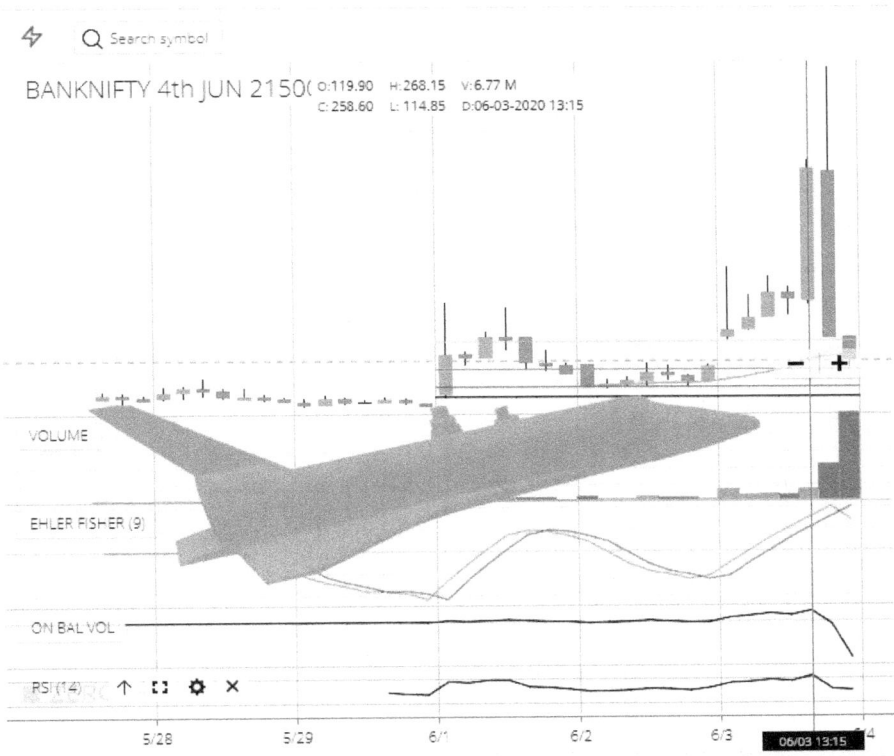

Here is another example of the same chart pattern which was captured on 4Th June 2020 which was a Thursday, you can observe, the time on the chart is 1:15 PM, and as usual after this formation of alternate small dotted candlestick patterns with alternate green and red colours, the option contract of 21500 CE of Bank Nifty flew up to give a huge move. So, it is as easy as to drink glass full of water. Just observe the chart pattern, see if it is the same as discussed and shown, if yes, then go for the trade. The profit taking and the risk is solely a trader's own decision, about which I won't be discussing much.

CHAPTER FOUR

Trading The Stock Options In The Month Expiry

As you have observed the huge moves taking place upon such unique chart pattern formation. The same is used to trade the stock options too in the Month's Expiry, the only difference is that, the pre-defined set of conditions differ here a bit. So, now we will be discussing about the conditions which must satisfy before we tend to take a trade in stock options.

Set of Conditions Which Must Be There For Trading Stock Options:

The following conditions are required before we initiate a trade in stock option:

- It should be the last week of that Particular Month, for example in this current month of July 2020, the expiry date is on 30/07/2020
- In general, the expiry week at the end of the month always witnesses a positive price action, so our focus will mostly be to trade the call options, however, if the chart pattern remains in favour then we might choose to buy put options
- The stock for which we would buy the option must be priced at least around Rupees 200 or above, that means the stock's price must be equal to or more than 200 Rupees
- For selecting the stock option, open the website **nseindia.com**, chose the F&O segment, see the list of stocks which are in top ten in terms of positive strength, out of them choose one or two which are most volatile in nature, that is, their daily price range is more than 10-15 points
- Add their call or put option in your watchlist, those call or put option must be at most 20 to 30 points distant from the stock's current price and their value must be somewhere between .1 rupee to .7 rupee, that is less than a Rupee

- See their chart pattern, if their chart pattern resembles to those of Bank Nifty and Nifty options which you saw in previous chapter, then you can take trades in them
- Always keep in mind, that there will always be risk associated with the trading, so you are not entitled to miss out the rule of not exceeding your losing limit
- Profit taking will depend upon your capacity to lose and of course your greed

Example:

In the last month, that is, June 2020, in the last week, when Indiabulls Housing Finance was trading at around 160 rupees, its call option at strike price point of 200 was priced at 1.2 rupees, and it had a lot size of 1200. So, let say if you would have bought 1200 quantities at around 1.50 Rupees, then the money engaged would have been 1800 Rupees, the same day it went up to 15 Rupees, so, if you would have sold it even 2 or 3 Rupees up from your buying price, you would have been in handsome profits. The next day it moved up to 57 Rupees, so, now you can imagine what potential these options have. But, what if the case would have been just the opposite? Then, the maximum loss you would have made would stand at 1800 Rupees only. Therefore, what we are risking is completely in our hand, do not forget to remember the size of your pocket while trading.

And what was observed in this stock? The same chart pattern, which I call "The Magical Pattern". So, whenever you do a research for finding a trade in options, just try to find such chart patterns, the time frame could be of 15 Minutes or even 1 Hour. The longer the time frame, the better the trading results.

The Uniqueness of My Strategy:

First of all, if you are a reader of my book then I congratulate you for your right decision for taking out your time. How much it was worth, that you will know yourself when you will take profit making trades in the market. While sharing with you, my "Holy Grail", neither I have been technical enough nor I discussed any complex terminology, but that doesn't mean I don't know them. I do know, but tell me, what a trader needs? Success or Hefty amount of knowledge which is worthless? I think, you are wise enough to understand. At the end of the chapter, I will leave you with some cautions, which you must take care of and at the same time I wish you all the best for your **Successful Trading Career**.

Risk Disclaimer

Think Before Risking Your Money In Stocks

It is known to one and all that trading in the stock market is rewarding, but at the same time it has the potential to take away all your hard earned money. These things have been sited well in advance in the beginning of the book. So, the readers are hereby informed that the trading strategies shared and the potential outcomes discussed were only meant to provide new traders with the right direction and to simplify their trading. But, my success doesn't gurantees your success too! Despite you got all in one working strategy, it will totally depend on individual's skill and capacity to use these strategies to their advantage. The readers are also requested to learn a bit more about the options so as to gain clarity while choosing trades in the live market. The author, under no any cicumstances irrespective of the geographical boundaries could be made accountable for any losses incurred by any individual who has been a reader of the book. The reader do not hold any right to raise any issue arising out of contents of the book. The application of the suggested trading idea is to the sole discretion of the reader and thus he/she themselves will be accountable for any losses taking place thereof.

www.ingramcontent.com/pod-product-compliance
Lightning Source LLC
Chambersburg PA
CBHW070847220526
45466CB00002B/918